CATS
of the
WILD

COUGARS

Henry Randall

PowerKiDS press™

New York

Published in 2011 by The Rosen Publishing Group, Inc.
29 East 21st Street, New York, NY 10010

First Edition

Editor: Joanne Randolph
Book Design: Ashley Burrell

Photo Credits: Cover © www.iStockphoto.com/Cathryn Thomas; p. 5 © www.iStockphoto.com/ John Pitcher; p. 6 Gerry Ellis/Getty Images; pp. 8–9, 13, 14, 17, 24 (right) iStockphoto/Thinkstock; p. 10 Stockbyte/Thinkstock; pp. 18–19 Martin Ruegner/Getty Images; pp. 20, 24 (left) © Bruce J. Lichtenberge/age fotostock; p. 23 Shutterstock.com; p. 24 (center left) Corbis Digital Vision; p. 24 (center right) Digital Vision.

Library of Congress Cataloging-in-Publication Data

Randall, Henry, 1972-
  Cougars / by Henry Randall. — 1st ed.
    p. cm. — (Cats of the wild)
  Includes bibliographical references and index.
  ISBN 978-1-4488-2516-5 (library binding) — ISBN 978-1-4488-2617-9 (pbk.) —
ISBN 978-1-4488-2618-6 (6-pack)
  1. Cougar—Juvenile literature. I. Title.
  QL737.C23.R358 2011
  599.75'24—dc22
                                      2010019789

Manufactured in the United States of America

CPSIA Compliance Information: Batch #WW11PK: For Further Information contact Rosen Publishing, New York, New York at 1-800-237-9932

Contents

Have you heard of cougars? Cougars are part of the cat family.

4

These wild hunters search for food in many different places. This cougar hunts in a forest.

This cougar lives in the **mountains**. Cougars are found from Canada to South America.

This cougar rests in a **rain forest** in South America. It waits for night to come so it can hunt for food.

Cougars have thick, tan fur. This fur keeps them warm in cold, snowy places.

This cougar shows off its sharp **teeth**. Cougars make many sounds but do not roar.

Cougars are good at climbing.
It can help them find animals
to hunt.

Cougars will swim to catch food, too. This cougar jumps into the water to find its dinner.

Cougar babies are called **cubs**. A cub stays with its mother for around two years.

Cougars are also called mountain lions or pumas.

Words to Know

cub

mountains

rain forest

teeth

Index

Web Sites

Due to the changing nature of Internet links, PowerKids Press has developed an online list of Web sites related to the subject of this book. This site is updated regularly. Please use this link to access the list:
www.powerkidslinks.com/cotw/cougars/